T0199192

PSALMS WARFARE OF PRAYERS:

The Lord is Mighty in Battle

———◆———

MINA PETERSEN

Copyright © 2021 Mina Petersen.

All rights reserved. No part of this book may be used or reproduced by any means, graphic, electronic, or mechanical, including photocopying, recording, taping or by any information storage retrieval system without the written permission of the author except in the case of brief quotations embodied in critical articles and reviews.

This book is a work of non-fiction. Unless otherwise noted, the author and the publisher make no explicit guarantees as to the accuracy of the information contained in this book and in some cases, names of people and places have been altered to protect their privacy.

WestBow Press books may be ordered through booksellers or by contacting:

WestBow Press
A Division of Thomas Nelson & Zondervan
1663 Liberty Drive
Bloomington, IN 47403
www.westbowpress.com
844-714-3454

Because of the dynamic nature of the Internet, any web addresses or links contained in this book may have changed since publication and may no longer be valid. The views expressed in this work are solely those of the author and do not necessarily reflect the views of the publisher, and the publisher hereby disclaims any responsibility for them.

Any people depicted in stock imagery provided by Getty Images are models, and such images are being used for illustrative purposes only.
Certain stock imagery © Getty Images.

Scriptures taken from the Holy Bible, New International Version®, NIV®. Copyright © 1973, 1978, 1984, 2011 by Biblica, Inc.™ Used by permission of Zondervan. All rights reserved worldwide. www.zondervan.com The "NIV" and "New International Version" are trademarks registered in the United States Patent and Trademark Office by Biblica, Inc.®

ISBN: 978-1-6642-2540-4 (sc)
ISBN: 978-1-6642-2541-1 (e)

Library of Congress Control Number: 2021903852

Print information available on the last page.

WestBow Press rev. date: 04/22/2021

WESTBOW
PRESS®
A DIVISION OF THOMAS NELSON
& ZONDERVAN

Why I wrote the book? Psalms Warfare Of Prayers The Lord Is Mighty In Battle

I truly love God's word. Psalms is one of my favorite book of the Old Testament in the Bible, and I really enjoy reading it almost everyday. I love it. Psalms is like my personal prayers book which I honestly treasure daily. Whenever I am going through spiritual battles of struggle in the storms of life feeling so distressed and overwhelmed. Psalms is the book I read to feel comfort and to feel the love of God speaking into my heart through the power of His Holy Spirit.

Contents

Introduction on Prayer

HOLY SPIRIT

Come, sweet precious Holy Spirit. I humbly, truly welcome you to invade the space of my dwelling place with your gentle presence. As I walk throughout this journey of life, empower me with your kindness of comfort. Enlighten my mind in the wisdom of your heart to be focused upon the things which are set above in Christ. Come Holy Spirit, strengthen every area of my weakness by your mighty power and fill me up. Come Holy Spirit, and baptize me with your healing, consuming fire of love. By the anointing of Jesus Christ of Nazareth, come Holy Spirit. Take charge over my spirit, my mind, my body, and help me to be fruitful and grow in the beauty of holiness. As a rushing wind, come Holy Spirit. Flow through me as a mighty river of water, so that my heart may rejoice with gladness all the days of my life in the eyes of my Heavenly Father, and in the pathway of His righteousness in Heaven. In Jesus' precious name, Amen.

CHAPTER

1

My Heart Is Joyful.......Psalm 30

Lord, the source of my strength, my heart calls upon Thee from morning to night. In the midst of my worship, I will pray and seek thy glorious presence of uprightness with Truth which enlightens my soul. The righteous may cry in their trouble of storm, but my God, you are my deliverance that is the joy which fills their heart. Therefore, their labor shall prosper, and bring foward bountiful, consistent harvests of fruits in due time. With trust and faith, they shall stand firm as a solid rock of a foundation on level ground that never fails. In Jesus' name, Amen.

For his anger lasts only a moment, but his favor lasts a lifetime; weeping may stay for the night but rejoicing comes in the morning. (Psalm 30:5) NIV

CHAPTER

2

You Are The Bread Which Filled My Soul.........Psalm 121

O eternal God, the ruler of all creation of heaven and earth, I lift up my head above which cometh the richest of foods with daily bread from the marvelous throne of Thy majestic glory and splendor.

(Psalms 121:1) Surely the righteous shall be satisfied because they honor Thy name with dignity and love; therefore, their soul will be enlightened and fulfilled with joy and prosperity all the days of their life. Thanks be to Thee, Lord Most High. In Jesus Christ name, Amen.

The Lord is good and He has compassion on all He has made. (Psalm 145:8) NIV

CHAPTER

3

You Have Defeated My Enemies...... ......Psalm 18

Blessed be thee, O Lord. Mighty One, hear the voice of my cry in the midst of darkness from my adversary. My God, my heart within me is overwhelmed because of pain and sorrow that seem to devour my soul. But Lord, my Redeemer, lift me up higher to a soild rock in victory that leads to everlasting joy. In you, my Lord, I will never be defeated, for you have made my hands to fight as a might lion of Judah that roars like a warrior soldier in war. Therefore, I love Thee, Lord my righteousness, for you are my anointing shield in all my battles(Psalm 18:1). Thank you my servant Lord, Amen.

Hear my cry, O God; listen to my prayer. (Psalm 61:1) NIV

CHAPTER

4

In You I Will Trust..........Psalm 27

O Lord in time of trouble, when I am surrounded by a storm of affliction, I will stand firm with gratitude and confidence, and with joyfulness in my heart. Almighty God, I put my trust in Thee. Turn not thy face far from thy servant of thy zion, but hearken unto the sincerity of my prayer in depression against my soul (Psalm 27:9). Lord, my shield, let not my enemies rule over me for they encamp about me. By thou victorious power of thy mighty hands, cast forward consuming coals upon them and let them be tormented; put to shame, perish, and die by the powerful blood of Jesus Christ of Nazareth. Amen.

Though an army besiege me, my heart will not fear; though war break out against me, even then I will be confident (Psalms 27: 3.) NIV

CHAPTER

5

I Will Forever Rejoice In You......Psalm 118

I will rejoice unto Thee, O God, with song of praise in the beauty of thy heavenly sanctuary. Blessed be Thy name, Thou Most High. Let not my enemies persecute me. Deliver me, my Lord, by Thy tender mercies in which my soul is saved.

(Psalms 118:24) Therefore, I shall not stumble into their ways of iniquity. But my heart will faithfully seek thy Truth and holiness of eternity that leads to the pathways of Thy Kingdom in heaven; from everlasting and to everlasting. In Jesus Christ's name, Amen.

Do not withhold your mercy from me Lord; may your love and faithfulness always protect me. (Psalm 40:11) NIV

CHAPTER

6

Forgive Me For My Sins........Psalm 51

My God, the light of my salvation, (Psalm 27:1) I come before thee in whom my soul delights, with a broken heart. (Psalm 51:17) Be compassionate unto me, O Lord, and forgive all of my sins. Cleanse me through your precious blood and take not thy Holy Spirit away from me, which my heart truly desires to honor and walk in humbleness and love.(Psalm 51:11) Lord, create within me thy free righteous spirit, and teach me to do that way of uprightness that lead to the throne of thy majestic glorious splendor. In Jesus name, Amen.

Teach me to do your will, for you are my God. By your good spirit, lead me on level ground. (Psalm 143:10) NIV

CHAPTER

7

My Enemies Is Powerless..........Psalm 35

Oh most High and mighty God, the rock of my strength, in Thee my heart glorifies thy holy name. (Psalm 86:9) Lord, forsaken me not in the face of my enemies without a cause. They set a trap against my soul in their secret hiding place. Therefore, my heart within me is afflicted. (Psalm 35:7) Be not silent my God, and let your angels of light strike them down with bow of arrows and flames of fire that they be scattered by force. Turn back in disgrace among themselves into a deep pit by the power of thy Holy Ghost. Let them be consumed and never rise back up again. In the mighty name of Jesus Christ, Amen.

Among the gods there is none like you, Lord; no deeds can compare with yours. (Psalms 86:8) NIV

8

You Come To My Rescue In Trouble.........Psalm 34

Glorious Lord, I cry unto Thee because of fear of disgrace that has overwhelmed me, and my spirit within me is desolate. Keep me from the violent men who seem to overthrow me in their wickedness (Psalm 140:4). Lord, many of the righteous are filled with the distraction of trouble (Psalm 34:19), but you rescue them all. Therefore, my soul exalts thee, Almighty, with joyful heart, and my lips continually will bless thee among all the heathen that walk in iniquity (Psalm 34:1). I will give thanks, O Lord, daily throughout all my days. In Jesus name, Amen.

So my spirit grows faint within me, and my heart within me is dismayed. (Psalm 86:8) NIV

CHAPTER

9

No Darkness Will Overshadow Me........Psalm 142

Lord, I lifted up my head unto Thee. My spirit within me is desolate in the sadness of my heart, but with thanks and gratitude I offer to you the incense of my prayer.

(Psalm 141:2) For thou art my portion, my deliverance in the land of evil men of darkness whose ways are mischievous. My God, for thy mercy's sake, cut them off with thy strong, mighty, victorious arm and scatter them with thy power. By consuming fire destroy them all in thy wrath. And may your lovingkindness bring my soul out of trouble. Draw closer unto me in comfort by thy tender love forever and forever. In Jesus' precious name, Amen.

Listen to my cry, for I am in desperate need. Rescue me from those who pursue me, for they are too strong for me. (Psalm 142:6) NIV

CHAPTER

10

In His Presence I am Still........Psalm 46

King of glory, my God, and my high tower and shield; for Thy name's sake, redeem me from the hand of men who work iniquity. In Thee I faithfully put my trust with strong confidence. Therefore, my heart within me is as still as a sweet voice of thy gentle, calm spirit.

(Psalm 46:10) My gracious Lord, my soul rests in peace with praise silently within my heart. Surely the righteous will be enlightened with songs of joy by the beauty of Thy holiness all their days. In Jesus Christ's name, Amen.

In you, Lord, I have taken refuge. Let me never be put to shame. Deliver me in your righteousness. (Psalm 31:1) NIV

CHAPTER

11

He Guides Me..........Psalm 31

My soul thirsts for thee Most High as a dry land. Be gracious unto me with compassion and attend to the request of my supplication in my cry. Hear me, O Lord, and have mercy upon me. Hide not Thy face from me in the midst of the wicked. By Thy righteous spirit, guide me; for they are stronger than I, but "Thou art my defense and refuge."(Psalm 31: 3) Therefore, leave not my soul in destitution by their destruction and iniquity. With gladness of joy, thy daughter of Zion will forever rejoice through the light of thy marvelous countenance of Thy glory. In Jesus holy name, Amen.

In your unfailing love, silence my enemies; destroy all my foes, for I am your servant. (Psalm 143: 12) NIV

Through The Darkest Valley...........Psalm 23

O God, the helper that comes to all my trouble, my heart within me is heavy in grief because of my adversary. They have cruel hatred against my soul with no cause. My Lord, for thy name's sake, deliver me. Let them not persecute me for Thou art my great shepherd of my rescue. With trust in Thee, though I walk down the road of the darkest valley in the midst of my enemies (Psalm 23:4), Thou shalt cover me with your holy blood, and shall preserve me and keep me alive as a delightful fruit in your sight (Psalm 17: 8). Under the armor of Thy light, I am filled with brightness and fire which is surrounded by walls of protection. Through the Holy Ghost and by thy victorious power of Thy anointing, I am saved forevermore in the glorious majesty of thy heavenly kingdom. In the mighty name of Jesus Christ of Nazareth, Amen.

Even though I walk through the darkest valley, I will fear no evil, for you are with me; your rod and your staff, they comfort me. (Psalm 23:4) NIV

"Psalm 23"

CHAPTER

13

The Righteous Will Treasure Your Wisdom.........Psalm 90

Lord, the salvation of my soul hears the voice of my distress in affliction of my heart. For thy mercy's sake, pull me out from men that walk in wolves' clothing, for their ways are deceitful and filled with corruption. I consider them as the enemies of my soul (Psalm 139:22). My God, let me not eat of their deadly poison. Surely the righteous will delight in the foundation of thy truth --in wisdom-- to the obedience of your commandments as a hidden treasure that grows within their hearts. Therefore, teach us to be mindful of how we live each day and to use our time wisely for your righteousness. Glory throughout eternity in heaven. (Psalm 90:12) In Jesus Christ's name, Amen.

Do not let my heart be drawn to what is evil so that I take part in wicked deeds along with those who are evildoers; do not let me eat their delicacies. (Psalm 141:4) NIV

CHAPTER

14

My Enemies Are consumed

My Jehovah Jireh, O King of all the universe, the Overcomer is mighty to save in whom my soul greatly takes refuge in battle of warfare (Psalm 24:8). Withhold not thy mercy from me throughout all my days for my trouble is enlarged because of the oppression of my enemies. They are so many; therefore, my heart within me is overwhelmed. Lord of my righteousness, attend to my hurt and let me not be ashamed in my integrity of uprightness in truth before thy presence. By force, let your holy angels of war drag them down into a dark pit with burning stones of fire and flames. Cast them in, and by the power of thy Holy Ghost let them burn into ashes forever. In the mighty name of Jesus Christ of Nazareth I pray, Amen.

The Lord protects and preserves them that are counted among the blessed in the land. He does not give them over to the desire of their foes. (Psalm 41:2) NIV

15

You Preserve Me..........Psalm 138

O Lord, the horn of my shield in whom I trust all my days; my strong tower. (Psalm 18:2) Though I walk in the midst of my trouble, Almighty One, Thou will preserve me in the face of my enemies. Thy right hand of your righteousness will protect me from the wrath of their destruction. (Psalm 138:7) Arise Most High my God, by force shoot out thy arrows of brimstone by fire and destroy them all by the power of thy Holy Ghost. Through thy spirit of uprightness, hide me under the shadow of your wings in your dwelling of the holy temple, thy majesty. In the mighty name of Jesus Christ, Amen.

Reach down your hand from on high; deliver me and rescue me from the mighty waters, and from the hands of foreigners whose mouths are full of lies; whose hands are deceitful. (Psalm 144:7) NIV

16

My Soul Is Redeemed

Father God, the Redeemer of my soul, everlasting Savior, in Thee my heart cries out in the midst of the wickedness of iniquity. Let them not rejoice over me that seem to take away the peace of thy righteousness in the glory of that heavenly kingdom. For thou art my portion of thy salvation, the rock of my defense; therefore, leave not my soul in the hand of bloody-guiltiness. Their ways are like vanity which devours; but my Lord, thou art greatly to be praised and thou mercy endures forever among all the heathen of all generations. (Psalm 24:8) By the anger of thy wrath; let burning coals of fire consume them, and by the anointing, victorious power of thy Holy Ghost, let them be destroyed. In the mighty name of Jesus Christ of Nazareth, Amen.

How long, Lord, will you look on? Rescue me from their ravages; my precious life from those lions. (Psalm 35:17) NIV

CHAPTER

17

I Give You All The Praise..........Psalm 86

Bow down Thy ear O God, and be merciful unto me in my distress, for you are the joy of my soul. In thee my heart greatly desires to walk in thy truth of your ways that lead to integrity. (Psalm 86:1) Lord, the righteous will give praise to thy name and will seek the face of your righteousness.(Psalm 86:11) My God, my buckler, you have anointed my head with thy oil of gladness in the day of tribulation. Therefore, when my enemies will turn back against me, send down hailstones of destruction and rushing wind. Let them stumble before thy presence and be confuse by force. Scattered them into their own evil ways forever. In Jesus' Christ's mighty name, Amen.

Though I walk in the midst of trouble, you preserve my life. You stretch out your hand against the anger of my foes; with your right hand you save me. (Psalm 138:7) NIV

CHAPTER

18

Let My Enemies Be Persecuted... ....

Servant Lord, Eternal Master, King of glory throughout all generations, Thou art my Refuge. Therefore, let not my soul be devoured by strong blooded men of iniquity who wish evil against me. Their hearts are filled with vanity and their lips speak of falsehood. Lord, rescue me in the midst of a horrible torment of confusion. By Thy righteous hand, uphold me with thy victorious arm. By thunder, let their ways tremble with great fear of destruction. Let thy warrior angels persecute them, and with flaming sword cut them all into pieces with your mighty strong hands. Cast them all in an oven of consuming, everlasting fire that never ends forevermore. In the mighty name of Jesus Christ of Nazareth, Amen.

May their path be dark and slippery with the angel of the Lord pursuing them (Psalm 35:6). NIV

CHAPTER

19

You Are My Comfort

I will exalt thee, my Lord, the keeper of my soul, in the midst of contentment from persecution and sorrow (Psalm 145:1). Thou art my hiding place of comfort and shield; therefore, sustain me from my adversary whose heart is filled with hatred. Their destiny is surrounded by violence. O Holy One of Israel, my anointing King of my salvation, in truth of Thou integrity, uphold me in the marvelous path of thy righteousness. Each day as I awake to seek Thy presence, my heart will surely magnify Thy name continually, and I shall rejoice and bless Thee with praise and honor of thy Heavenly kingdom. In Jesus Christ's name, Amen.

Teach me your way, Lord, and lead me in a straight path because of my oppressors (Psalm 27:11). NIV

CHAPTER
20

I Will Bless My God Forever

My Lord, the God of Abraham, Isaac, and Jacob, I will bless thee, and with joyful lips I will honor Thy name; my Redeemer and the Creator of my salvation. Therefore, I have not despised thy righteous commandments within my heart before the face of ungodly men of iniquity. They speak words of hatred in deceitfulness, and their tongue is as sharp as a two-edge sword which worketh wickedness. Lord, by thy right hand break every false tooth in their mouth and let their language be confounded among themselves that seem to devise my hurt. By the wrath of thy breath, blow around about their dwelling place from the throne of Thou glorious kingdom. Cast upon them heavy coals of fire with the thunder of lightning. By Thy mighty strong arm bring them down into a pit of destruction and let them perish. In the mighty name of Jesus Christ I pray, Amen.

LORD, how many are my foes? How many rise up against me? (Psalm 3:1) NIV

CHAPTER
21

Count Me Blameless.........Psalm 139

Almighty God, my Deliverance, Thou art familiar with all my path (Psalms 139: 3). Even when my feet slip into a prison of iniquity with corruption, surrounded by a wall of darkness in the midst of the heathen, or whether I am oppressed with affliction, thou truly does know every word within my heart.

(Psalms 139:2) Therefore, because of thy tender mercies in which my soul takes delight; I shall not be consumed, but Thou marvelous light of uprightness of your salvation shines from your holy hill in heaven above. You will surely enlighten me with thou garment of glory. By the anointing victory of thy Holy Ghost, I shall walk blameless as a living sacrifice before the holy temple of thy righteousness. Lord, the prince of peace causes the wind of the storm to be still, but Thou dost dwell among the righteous of zion, and I will faithfully rejoice. In Jesus Christ's mighty name, Amen.

If I go up to the heavens, you are there; if I make my bed in the depths, you are there (Psalm 139:8). NIV

CHAPTER
22

My Shield That Stands High

Redeem me, Most High Lord of Israel, from the hand of strange, unjust, bloody men whose hearts within them have rebelled against the law of thy covenant of uprightness. They have dug a horrible deep ditch for my soul in the midst of the dark wilderness where wolves and wild beasts and all kind of creatures live that devour. Therefore, because of thy steadfast love, let me not fall into the net of their evil acts of mischievousness. For thou art greatly my Refuge. I shall not be moved; neither shall my heart fear (Psalm 55:22). Thou shalt surrounded me with Thy wing of your protection before their face and with the strong arm of Thy righteousness. Through the power of thy Holy Ghost, let your angels of battle destroy them all by consuming fire. In the mighty name of Jesus Christ, Amen.

Lead me Lord in your righteousness. Because of my enemies, make your way straight before me (Psalm 5:8) NIV

CHAPTER

23

He Is My Protection..........Psalm 91

Hearken unto my prayer O Lord, my Jehovah Jireh. The silent within me is overwhelming, but thou shalt comfort me with song of joy day-by-day by thy victorious spirit. In the midst of the storm and in the time of my battle, you are there. By thy mercy, which extends throughout the holy hill in heaven, you comfort me. Therefore, holiness will sustain my soul by thy right hand from every deadly evil poison of pestilence.

(Psalms 91:10) That is hidden in the darkness of danger will not gather against me even in the night of my dwelling, because thou shalt cover me with your precious and holy blood. For Thou art the God of my righteousness and the Rock of my refuge. The shadow of thy glory shall encamp above me as a shield-- like a strong tower that stands high and never fades away forever. In the mighty name of Jesus Christ of Nazareth, Amen.

A thousand may fall at your side ten thousand at your right hand, but it will not come near you. (Psalm 91:7) NIV

"Psalm 91"

24

Tribulation In The Battle Ground

Lord of hosts, Servant Master in whom my soul takes pleasure daily with steadfastness in my heart, I will surely magnify Thy name in the midst of the heathen whose lips speaks of iniquity. For Thou art truly my armor of shelter, and my Buckler among the living of Zion. O my God, you are the Rock of my deliverance in trouble and I am filled with contentment-- with joy and peace from above-- which passes thy understanding. In Thee Lord, you shall surrounded my dark battle under thy victorious wings of the anointing by Thy Holy Ghost. The light which shines from the secret place above thou tabernacle has enlightened the darkness throughout my valley before the face of all my enemies. Thou shalt uphold me in the palm of thy hand of uprightness forever. In the precious name of Jesus Christ, Amen.

You make your saving help my shield and your right hand sustains me. Your help has made me great. (Psalm 18:35) NIV

CHAPTER

25

Tribulation In The Storm

Eternal Father, Prince of Peace my comforted, Lord hear the secret of my prayer in the midst of my cry throughout the shadow of darkness in tribulation of the valley in the storm. O Most High withhold not that tender mercies from me, but for thy goodness' sake, rescue me for thou art truly mighty to save my soul from all evil and the satanic persecutor of iniquity. In time of the battlefield of oppression from the hand of my enemies, sent against me to distract my confidence and hope, I am trusting in Thee day and night; every moment of each day. My heart is committed to great dignity and integrity; therefore, I will walk in the light of thy marvelous righteousness with steadfastness. With joy of praise I am filled with gratitude. I shall glorify thy holy name of truth forever before the beautiful gate of Zion that leads to eternity from above thy sanctuary at the kingdom of your holiness. Throughout all the days of my life, I will surely seek for Thy salvation. In Jesus Christ mighty name, Amen.

I call to you, . Come quickly to me; hear me when I call to you. May my prayer be sent before you like incense; may the lifting up of my head be like the evening sacrifice. (Psalm 141:1) NIV

CHAPTER

26

Battleground In The Battlefield

Great is thy faithfulness, mighty God our Lord. Over all generations of Zion, which my heart so cherishes greatly, I am truly honored in the midst of war-filled where there is corruption and violence in the valley of dark tribulation. It seems to be gathered by heathen men of the world, and their pathway is working in iniquity. O Lord Almighty, count me blameless among the light of the righteous which walk uprightly from thy holy mountain in heaven above. God of my protection and strong refuge, let not my soul drift toward any evil acts of their wickedness, but by thy wrath, let them be terrified horribly and put to shame into madness. Send thy group of angels marching like soldiers in battle to encamp around their secret tent of dwelling with swords of fire. By force, let them all be slaughtered and cast them to that hungry beast which devours as a wild lion that lives in complete darkness forever. In the mighty name of Jesus Christ of Nazareth I pray, Amen.

For great is your love toward me; you have delivered me from the depths, from the realm of the dead. (Psalm 86:13) NIV

CHAPTER
27

Victory Belongs To The Lord

Good Shepherd, Eternal God, in Thee my soul magnifies Thy salvation of your glory from high above the holy temple of Your Heavenly Kingdom. Therefore, my heart within me is steadfast in the midst of confusion from my enemies of iniquity. O Lord, by Thy spirit of uprightness, stretch out Thy hand and shoot out ten thousand brimstones of fire against them. Lord let them be devoured by Thy Holy Ghost and be consumed away into a pit below a danger ground of a torment that never ends. My righteous God, I bless Thee. You have given me the victory to overcome every stepping stone of disgrace. You have sharpened the surface of my weapon for war as a sharp blade--like a quiver of arrows--into two-edge swords that destroy every evil force of darkness. Praise be unto Thee, Most High of Israel. In the mighty name of Jesus Christ, Amen.

He trains my hands for battle, and my arms can bend a bow of bronze. (Psalm 18:34) NIV

CHAPTER

28

I Will Walk In His Light Of Truth

O mighty God, you are the blameless Lion of Judah that comes to my rescue in temptation, and trials of war. Therefore, the faithful righteous which treasure thy steadfast love within their heart shall truly honor Thy glorious, marvelous name which stands way above all evildoers that live in the deceitful land of iniquity; like as in the day of Sodom and Gomorrah. But in Thee, O Lord, thou art the Rock that stands around my shelter in battle of trouble by thy Holy Ghost of my comfort. And the salvation of thy true light will uphold my soul through all eternity. My holy God, my heart is grateful forever and stilled with praise unto thee. In Jesus Christ's precious name, Amen.

"Because he loves me," says the Lord, "I will rescue him. I will protect him for he acknowledges my name." (Psalm 91:14) NIV

29

I Will Truly Walk In Integrity Of His Commandments

Lord, my Stronghold and Fortress; my soul is enlightened by the light of Thy victorious anointing spirit of glory which dwells in heaven into the throne of your majestic, glorious splendor. Throughout the land of the righteous that walk in true statutes of Thy holy commandments, my heart leaps for joy in Thy integrity of Thy righteousness. I will not be moved or oppressed, but I shall surely sacrifice my life to behold the face of Thy uprightness among all of the vanity of the heathen of darkness. In the mighty name of Jesus Christ, Amen.

The law of the LORD is perfect refreshing the soul. The statutes of the LORD are trustworthy, making wise the simple. (Psalm 19:7) NIV

30

His Lovingkindness Is Everlasting..........Psalm 136

O praise the Lord and rejoice all ye saints of Zion who delight in his righteousness. Give thanks unto his glorious name above his heavenly sanctuary, for his lovingkindness is everlasting. Pour out your soul and sing a new song within your heart daily--with joyfulness--all ye people, and walk uprightly, for his lovingkindness is everlasting. He has redeemed us from all deadly affliction of diseases in darkness, and He has delivered us for His mercy' sake by His victorious power. His lovingkindness is everlasting. He has forgiven us for all our sins of iniquity by shedding His precious blood on the cross in the day of redemption. His lovingkindness is everlasting. He comforts us with his faithful love, and by His grace He sustains us when our spirits are overwhelmed in the midst of persecution from the battle of the enemies. His loving-kindness is everlasting. He shields us with his armor of salvation in glory, so we will not be misled into the dark path of destruction. His lovingkindness is everlasting. O bless the Lord. Bless His mighty, holy name throughout the ends of all the earth. His loving-kindness is everlasting. Amen and Amen!

Give thanks to the Lord for He is good. His love endures forever. (Psalm 136:1) NIV